W9-AWL-763

WORLD ATLAS

Written by NICK CRANE
Illustrated by DAVID DEAN

Barefoot Books
step inside a story

Contents

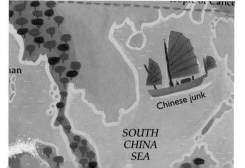
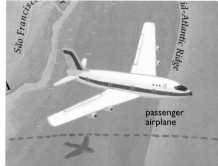

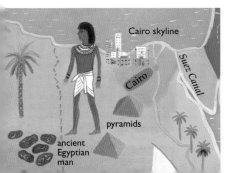

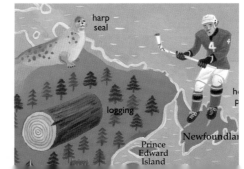
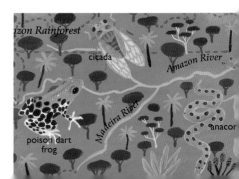

The Story of Our Planet

The Solar System

An atlas is the most recent chapter of a miracle story. It is a story that began when a small part of the universe collapsed to form a dense core surrounded by a rotating disc of gas and dust particles. Nearly all of the material in the swirling disc ended up being drawn to the core, where it formed a shining sphere, the sun. The scattered grains of remaining material collided with each other and eventually formed the family of planets that we call the solar system, with the sun at its center.

Pluto

Saturn

Mercury Sun Venus

Neptune

Mars Earth

Jupiter

Uranus

One of these planets, the one third-closest to the sun, was destined to be different. It was so hot that it was molten. When it started to cool, a crust formed on its outside, rather like a cracked shell. Very, very slowly, parts of the crust slid across the surface of the planet. When they collided, their edges sometimes bent and folded into ranges of mountains. Cracks opened up, allowing molten rock and gasses to escape upwards as volcanoes of heat and gas, creating new landscapes.

The First Signs of Life

All the while, this ball of spinning rock was being bombarded by meteorites and comets — some of which carried water or ice. Eventually, warm, soupy oceans covered most of the planet's surface, which became wrapped in a thin film of gases — the beginnings of an atmosphere. Nobody knows for sure, but it is likely that the first forms of life, bacteria, developed deep in the planet's scalding interior through a series of chemical reactions. It took ages for the earliest, simplest life forms to migrate from the depths to the bright sunlight of the surface. Bacteria evolved into multicellular organisms, which evolved into plants and worms, fish, amphibians, reptiles, insects, birds and mammals.

The Human Species

When the planet was pulverized by meteorites, or clouded by volcanic eruptions, whole species were wiped out; others adapted. One of these species eventually learned to run, climb and swim. It also developed a complex mind which was curious about technology, art and music. This species had a sense of what was "right" and what was "wrong." It spent a lot of time just thinking about things. *Homo sapiens* (a Latin name meaning "wise human") inherited a planet of incredible diversity. The oceans teemed with fish. The great mountain ranges poured with rivers of crystal water, fed by snowfields and glaciers. Forests reached across entire land masses. When humans learned to measure time, they discovered that 4,700 million years had passed since their home first started to take shape. We now estimate that our species has been around for only 140,000 years. If you think of the life of the planet as a week, we have been here for less than one minute!

Mapping the World

The Story of Mapmaking

The first book of maps to carry the title "Atlas" was created in the sixteenth century by Gerard Mercator, who was born in Flanders, now Belgium. An atlas is both a precise geometric and an artistic way of representing the different features of the world on paper. The way in which people design atlases is influenced by many factors, including the knowledge they have about the physical features and distances within the different regions; what aspects of life are culturally, economically and politically significant to them; and what geometric techniques they have mastered.

Atlases are a compromise, because it is impossible to flatten the planet, which is a three-dimensional sphere, into two dimensions without distorting the geography. Over the centuries, mapmakers, or cartographers, have created new, two-dimensional projections of the earth to try to resolve this problem. Ever since the earliest navigators set sail, we have been making discoveries about our planet and the universe. But no atlas can be accurate for long: the planet is a living, changing place and there is still a lot about it that we do not know.

About this Atlas

The maps in this atlas describe the planet as it is today and illustrate some of the ways in which people in different parts of the world are trying to achieve a better balance between humans and the environment. There is a lot more sea than land on the planet and the sea is far less well known than much of the land.

The first maps in this atlas explore this relatively uncharted territory, from the biggest of the major oceans, the Pacific, to the Southern Ocean. Next, the maps lead you on a journey from east to west, starting in Oceania, where the International Date Line is situated.

Some atlases divide the world by continent. This atlas is divided by region, with an emphasis on the way in which people in different parts of the world have been influenced by the physical characteristics of the land and by the resources around them. Until recently, human beings have lived on the planet in a relatively sustainable way, seldom taking more than can be replaced by natural growth. But in the past century, this balance has changed. Each region has its own story and today some human beings live in a more sustainable way than others, but all of the regions are connected to each other like the pieces of a jigsaw. We are living at the start of a new chapter in the story of our planet and its central theme is the way in which we work together as a global community to protect it.

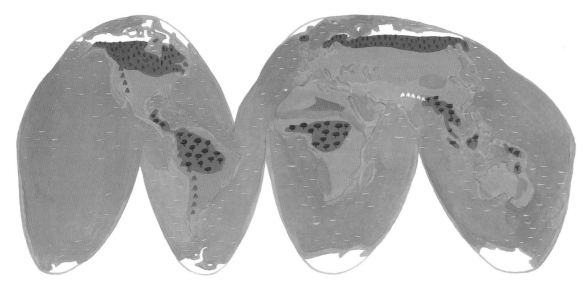

Goode Homolosine Projection:
This type of projection has the least distortion. It is sometimes referred to as a "peeled orange" because it is as if the surface of the globe has been "peeled" and flattened.

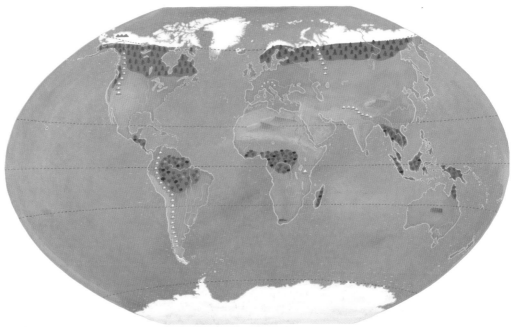

Winkel Tripel Projection:
This projection provides a good balance between a globe-like shape and a true representation of the areas of the world. This is the projection used for the world map on the next page.

ARCTIC

NORTH
AMERICA

ATLANTIC
OCEAN

PACIFIC
OCEAN

SOUTH
AMERICA

Continents of the World

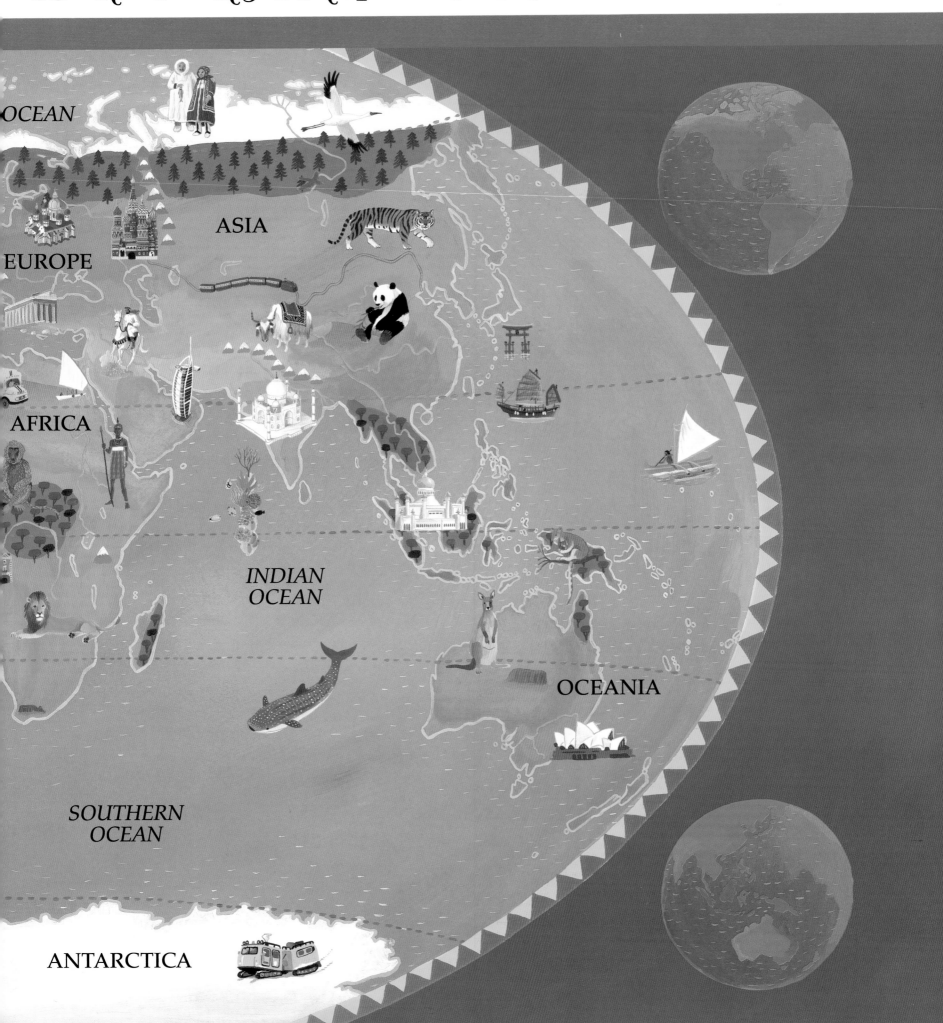

OCEAN

EUROPE

ASIA

AFRICA

INDIAN
OCEAN

OCEANIA

SOUTHERN
OCEAN

ANTARCTICA

The Oceans

Oceans have far more in common with each other than continents, because they are all connected. Currents flow between them, mixing their waters.

You could say that there is just one big ocean. However, people tend to divide them into five: the Pacific, Atlantic, Indian, Arctic and Southern Oceans.

The oceans are much more mysterious than landmasses. Even today, they are not fully explored. We know that they contain nearly all the water on earth (97%) but we don't know much about life in the oceans. Scientists estimate that they provide a habitat for 80% of life on Earth: perhaps as many as 10 million different species live in the oceans, only 300,000 of them recorded.

Most of the earth's incoming solar radiation is absorbed by the oceans, which store thermal energy extremely effectively. Ocean currents play a major role in distributing heat around the globe, making them key elements in the climate system.

About 73% of the world's fish supply comes from the oceans. Altogether, fish provide some 2.8 billion people with at least one-fifth of their protein intake. Since the 1950s, the increasing amounts of fish being caught in our oceans have drastically reduced stocks and threaten to make many species extinct. Today, governments and international organizations are working together to coordinate fishing policy and protect fish stocks. However, no single body controls fishing in international waters, so voluntary cooperation between countries and their fishing fleets is essential.

Oceans can be crossed by many different means. Ferdinand Magellan's expedition (1519–22) was the first to sail around the world. His flagship, *Trinidad*, led a fleet of five ships provided by King Charles V. Other pioneering ocean crossings include Charles Lindbergh's solo flight by monoplane in 1927 across the Atlantic Ocean. Amelia Earhart was the first woman to repeat Lindbergh's feat, exactly five years later. In 1981, *Double Eagle V* became the first balloon to cross the Pacific Ocean.

BERING SEA

bowhead whale

volcanoes ("The Ring of Fire")

SEA OF OKHOTSK

Aleutian Trench

sea otter

ASIA

Pacific herring

Kuril Trench

International Date Line

SEA OF JAPAN

Japan Trench

giant squid

Hawaiian Islands (USA)

athyscaphe *Trieste*

bluefin tuna

outrigger canoe

Marianna Trench

Double Eagle V

PACIFIC

dfish

great frigatebird

canoe

beaked whale

Solomon Islands

leatherback turtle

Fiji Islands

Great Barrier Reef

CORAL SEA

Tonga Trench

OCEANIA

Taranaki natural gas field

TASMAN SEA

bottlenose dolphin

SOUTHERN OCEAN

Yukon River

GULF OF
ALASKA

salmon

container
ship

sea lion

Great Pacific
Garbage Patch

OCEAN

yelloweye
rockfish

seaplane

Kon-Tiki

Tuamotu Islands
(France)

Cook Islands

Tahiti

Easter Island statues

freighter

killer whale

Easter Island
(Chile)

iceberg

NORTH AMERICA

HUDSON
BAY

MEXICO,

The Pacific Ocean

The largest ocean is the Pacific, which occupies about one-third of the globe. It is greater in extent than the total land area of the world.

Physical Features

The Pacific has over 25,000 islands, which is more than all the other oceans combined, although the islands are mostly tiny. The Asian side of the ocean is broken into huge islands and peninsulas, and into several seas: the South China Sea, East China Sea, Yellow Sea, Sea of Japan, Sea of Okhotsk and Bering Sea.

The deepest part of the Pacific is also the lowest point on the planet. Between Japan and New Guinea, where the boundary between two of the earth's crustal plates has created an underwater chasm called the Mariana Trench, the depth is 35,827ft. If you dropped Mount Everest into this, it would still be covered by 6,562ft of water.

Climate and Weather

Temperatures in the Pacific Ocean range from below 32°F in the polar areas to 86°F at the equator. Periodically, parts of the tropical Pacific warm by a few degrees Fahrenheit, which can have a huge effect on the earth's climate. This phenomenon, called El Niño, can cause extreme weather like floods and droughts in many different parts of the world.

Natural Resources

The Pacific Ocean is home to all kinds of fish, including herring, salmon, sardines, snapper, swordfish and tuna. Many shellfish also live in its waters, as do larger sea creatures such as dolphins, turtles and whales. The ocean has rich reserves of gas and oil, providing energy for Australia, New Zealand, China, Peru and the United States.

Environment

Oil pollution and overfishing threaten many marine species in the Pacific Ocean, particularly whales, turtles, seals, sea otters, sea lions and the strange dugong, or "sea cow," which eats coastal plants and can live for up to 70 years.

In the north Pacific floats the Great Pacific Garbage Patch, which is an enormous area of plastic waste. This kills more than a million seabirds each year and as many marine animals. International efforts are being made to clear it up.

The Atlantic Ocean

The Atlantic Ocean is just over half the size of the Pacific and the second largest of the world's oceans. It reaches from the Arctic Ocean in the north to the Southern Ocean in the south.

Physical Features

Compared to the Pacific, the Atlantic doesn't have many islands, but around its edges there are a number of shallow seas, like the Caribbean, the Gulf of Mexico, the Mediterranean, the Baltic and the Black Sea.

The Atlantic was created when the continents of Africa and North and South America began drifting apart about 130 million years ago. Deep beneath its surface is a mountain range called the Mid-Atlantic Ridge, where molten lava has risen through the rupture in the ocean floor caused by the earth's plates moving apart. Today, the Atlantic Ocean is still growing wider, at a rate of about one inch a year.

Climate and Weather

Sea-surface temperatures in the Atlantic vary. Around the equator, temperatures reach up to 83°F, while in the polar regions they sink to around 44°F. Average temperatures have risen by 1.26°F over the last century.

Ocean currents influence the climate: the Gulf Stream brings warm waters to northwest Europe, while cold currents create dense fog off the coasts of eastern Canada and northwest Africa.

Natural Resources

The Atlantic is the world's richest source of fish. Common species are cod, haddock, hake, herring and mackerel. The rocks below the ocean bed are rich in oil and gas, and sand and gravel banks provide raw materials for the building industry.

Environment

To the west and east of the Atlantic are the two continents — North America and Europe — which have emitted well over half of the world's greenhouse gases. The major greenhouse gases generated by human activity are carbon dioxide and methane. Growth in atmospheric carbon concentration (over 25% since the mid 1800s) is mainly due to our use of fossil fuels.

The oceans play a vital role in absorbing carbon dioxide and maintaining the planet's carbon balance. Half of the carbon dioxide generated by human beings since 1800 has been absorbed by the sea. However, so much carbon dioxide is being absorbed by the oceans that it is increasing the acidity of the water and destroying many forms of marine life.

Did You Know?

Marine Life

There are nearly 6 million Atlantic puffins in the North Atlantic. Atlantic puffins can fly and swim, sometimes diving over 200ft underwater to catch the small fish they eat. Although penguins are also birds, they cannot fly. Millions of Magellanic penguins live along the coasts of Argentina and Chile, but they are still classified as a threatened species due to the oil spills that kill thousands each year off the coast of Argentina.

Transport

Transatlantic exploration has brought European and African culture to the Americas. Over 1,000 years ago, Icelander Leif Ericson was the first European to discover North America's coastline. In 1952, Ann Davison became the first woman to sail across the Atlantic single-handed in her 23-foot boat, *Felicity Ann*. Hundreds of commercial flights cross the Atlantic every day, and the ocean continues to be a major route for sea freight.

The Indian Ocean

The Indian Ocean is just under half the size of the Pacific and is enclosed on three sides by the continents of Africa, Asia and Australia.

Physical Features

The Indian Ocean is split into three basins by an underwater mountain range which is known as an oceanic ridge. The ridge was formed millions of years ago by the meeting of three of the earth's crustal plates. At 23,819ft deep, the Java Trench is the deepest point of this ocean. Madagascar, which lies to the east of the coast of Africa, is the fourth-largest island in the world.

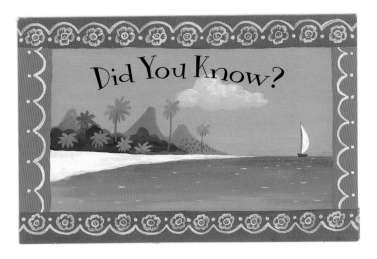
Did You Know?

Climate and Weather

Much of the Indian Ocean lies in the tropics, so it is the warmest of the oceans. Its tropical climate has a strong effect on the surrounding continents. During the seasonal monsoons, moist air collects over the ocean and falls as torrential rain in countries like Pakistan, India and Bangladesh. Northeast India is the rainiest place on Earth, while high temperatures have turned the Red Sea into one of the saltiest seas in the world.

Natural Resources

Around 40% of the world's offshore oil production is based in the Indian Ocean. As a consequence, marine life in the Arabian Sea, the Persian Gulf and the Red Sea is being affected by pollution from the oil wells.

The Indian Ocean region has the largest number of active fishermen in the world. There is a wide range of marine life for fishermen to catch, including tuna, sardines and shrimp. Attracted by the wealth from oil and fishing, piracy has increased on the Indian Ocean, although governments from around the globe are working together to make the ocean safer for merchants.

Environment

The warming of the oceans through climate change will have a particularly high impact in the Indian Ocean. As the temperature of the oceans rises, their volume increases too, causing sea levels to rise. This means that the many people who live on the low-lying shores of the Indian Ocean may have to move inland.

Marine Life

The warm water of the Indian Ocean is less suitable for marine life than that of the cooler oceans, because there are fewer nutrients for the microscopic plants, known as phytoplankton, which are the beginning of the marine food chain. Many whale sharks live in the warm waters of the Indian Ocean, though they migrate all over the world. These sharks feed primarily on plankton. They are the largest fish in the sea, sometimes over 39ft long, the size of an average bus.

Whale sharks are a threatened species, as are dugongs, large mammals that may have inspired the earliest mermaid tales. Dugongs look similar to manatees and are an easy target for coastal hunters who seek their meat and oil. Other species in danger of extinction are seals, turtles and whales.

Transport

For thousands of years, the Indian Ocean has been a water highway between Africa and Asia. The traditional trading vessel in the western part of the ocean was the Arabian dhow, a slender wooden craft with a triangular lateen sail. By contrast, today's merchant ships, which carry containers, are powered by fossil fuels rather than relying on wind and current. A huge increase in worldwide trade has meant increases in carbon emissions from shipping. In 2005, twice as much food was traded around the world as in 1990.

SOUTHWEST ASIA

EAST ASIA

MEDITERRANEAN SEA

cruise liner

Suez Canal

Nile River

PERSIAN GULF

Indus River

Himalayas

Yangtze River

YELLOW SEA

RED SEA

Ganges River

SOUTHEAST ASIA

Tropic of Cancer

ARABIAN SEA

oil rig

NORTH AFRICA

mackerel

scuba diver

Andaman Islands (India)

Chinese junk

coral reef

SOUTH CHINA SEA

Arabian dhow

Equator

hawksbill turtle

tsunami

angelfish

Mt. Kilimanjaro

SEYCHELLES

MALDIVES

JAVA SEA

Java Trench

COMOROS

Mid-Indian Ridge

underwater government meeting

Christmas Islands (Australia)

Zambezi River

MAURITIUS

INDIAN OCEAN

MADAGASCAR

Réunion (France)

SOUTHERN AFRICA

dugong

Tropic of Capricorn

OCEANIA

sardines

whale shark

Amsterdam Island (France)

southern bluefin tuna

seals

Southwest Indian Ridge

Southeast Indian Ridge

passenger airplane

SOUTHERN OCEAN

container ship

icebreaker

Antarctic Circle

The Arctic Ocean

The Arctic is by far the smallest and shallowest of the world's oceans; it is 18 times smaller than the Pacific with an average depth of 3,445ft. It is almost completely surrounded by North America, Europe and north Asia.

Physical Features

The center of the Arctic Ocean is occupied by a layer of ice about 10ft thick. The Arctic is not as cold as Antarctica, because the seawater beneath the Arctic ice is warmer than the land beneath the Antarctic ice. The Arctic Ocean is connected to the Pacific by the 32 mile-wide Bering Strait, and to the Atlantic by the much broader Greenland Sea.

The northernmost point on Earth, the North Pole, is about 435 miles from the coast of northern Greenland. Most of this ice is continuously in motion, breaking into different pieces and drifting around. In 1937, the Soviet Union launched the first temporary drift-ice station, "North Pole-1," which allowed them to explore its Arctic without needing to leave the base. The drift stations research ice, oceanology, marine biology, meteorology and more.

Climate and Weather

The Arctic Ocean is a region of dark, cold winters and short, cool summers: in summer, temperatures rise to 32°F and in winter they fall to −40°F. At the North Pole, the sun is permanently below the horizon during the winter months and permanently above it during the summer months.

Natural Resources

Oil and gas companies are considering tapping into the rich resources of the Arctic seabed, where there may be as much as 13% of the world's undiscovered oil and 30% of its undiscovered gas. Sand and gravel aggregates, as well as fish, can all be found in abundance in the Arctic Ocean.

Environment

Of all the oceans, the Arctic is most affected by climate change. In recent decades, some parts of the Arctic Ocean have warmed by more than 5°F. Almost half the ice has disappeared since satellite observations began in 1979, and scientists warn that by 2040, the entire ocean may be free of ice in summer. The disappearance of the Arctic ice will affect the ocean's fragile ecosystem and will also accelerate global warming because open water absorbs heat from the sun, whereas ice reflects it back. So, taking action to reduce climate change is vital to the survival of the many species that live in and around the Arctic.

Did You Know?

Wildlife

Many creatures have adapted to the Arctic climate. Polar bears have large, furry feet to help distribute their weight on thin ice, while their white fur has hollow hairs, which trap air and help insulate them from the cold. A less familiar Arctic mammal is the narwhal, also known as the unicorn whale due to its 6-foot-long tusk.

Snowy owls live on the Arctic tundra but are unlike other owls as they hunt during the day instead of at night. In the winter, snowy owls are completely white, but their plumage changes to brown in the summer, acting as camouflage. Other animals inhabiting the Arctic include snow geese, tundra swans, peregrine falcons, grizzly bears, musk oxen, gray wolves and arctic foxes.

Transport

The Northwest Passage is a route through the Arctic which links the Atlantic and the Pacific. After several unsuccessful attempts in the nineteenth century, the Passage was finally navigated in 1906 by the explorer Roald Amundsen in a 47-ton fishing boat, the *Gjøa*. He and his crew spent three successive winters trapped in pack ice.

Antarctica and the Southern Ocean

The world's third-smallest continent is almost twice the size of the United States, but it has the population of a village.

Physical Features

Antarctica is a land of ice. In places, the ice is nearly 16,404ft thick, and in total it accounts for about 90% of the world's fresh water. Less than 1% of Antarctica is free of ice. Buried beneath the ice are entire mountain ranges. Antarctica is the highest continent on Earth, which is one of the reasons that it is so cold and windy. The Southern Ocean was formed when Antarctica and South America moved apart about 30 million years ago.

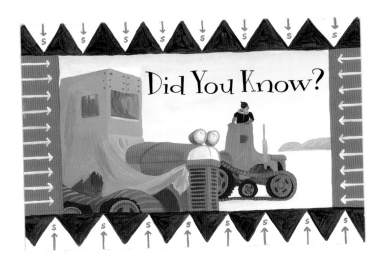

Did You Know?

Climate and Weather

The annual mean temperature on the Antarctic Plateau is around -69°F, which makes it the coldest place in the world. It is also the windiest, with wind speeds on the coast reaching about 200mph during gales. Rising sea temperatures have caused the Antarctic Peninsula to become 5.4°F warmer over the last 50 years. Antarctica is also the world's driest continent: there are places where rain has not fallen for 2 million years.

Natural Resources

Antarctica has reserves of coal, gas and iron ore. Mining is prohibited under the Antarctic Treaty of 1959. Some of its waters are fished for krill, finfish and crab, but quotas are carefully controlled.

Environment

Nobody owns Antarctica. Under the terms of the Antarctic Treaty, the entire continent is a peaceful, non-militarized land open to scientific research and controlled tourism. As one of the world's most important natural laboratories, it is vital to understanding the planet's ocean and climate systems. It is the only continent that has never been permanently settled by human beings, but up to 5,000 scientists occupy a scattering of research stations, mostly on the coast. The most isolated of these stations is the Vostok Station, founded in 1957. It sits on top of a large subglacial lake, which is under 13,123ft of ice.

By drilling 2.5 miles into the Antarctic ice, scientists have been able to obtain a record of the earth's climate going back 800,000 years. These records show that the level of carbon dioxide released into the earth's atmosphere has soared dramatically since the Industrial Revolution. Greenhouse gases (such as carbon dioxide) trap heat in the atmosphere causing a rise in the earth's temperature. This is known as global warming or the greenhouse effect.

Wildlife

The creature most often associated with Antarctica is the penguin. Of the 18 species of penguin in the world, 4 breed in Antarctica: the Adélie, emperor, chinstrap and gentoo penguins. Penguins cannot fly but they are superb swimmers. They spend about 75% of their time in the water but they breed on land or on sea ice in huge colonies known as rookeries.

The other notable bird of this region is the albatross. These large sea birds are able to cover huge distances without resting. The great albatross has the widest wingspan of any living bird. Albatrosses are under threat due to overfishing, pollution and also longline fishing.

Transport

The extremely low temperatures and continuous winds make traveling in Antarctica especially difficult. Transport is further limited by environmental concerns: it is important to avoid disrupting the ecosystem or polluting the region. Today, most transport is conducted via water or air, though skis, snowshoes and snowmobiles are also used for overland travel.

Oceania

If you spin a globe until it looks as if it's mostly covered by sea, you'll be looking at Oceania. Only 33 million people live here — 20 million of them in Australia, 3.7 million in New Zealand and 9.3 million in the islands of the South Pacific.

Pacific Islands

Physical Features
There are between 20,000 and 30,000 islands in the Pacific. New Guinea is the largest landmass in the area, covering 488,398 square miles, though half of it extends into southeast Asia. At the other end of the scale, there are numerous uninhabited coral atolls and mountainous islands covered in lush, tropical rainforest.

People and Places
The small islands of Oceania are incredibly varied. The tribal groups of Papua New Guinea speak 820 different languages, while the Federated States of Micronesia occupy 607 islands. Suva is the capital and largest city of Fiji.

Climate and Weather
The weather in this region is tropical all year round, with a hotter and more humid period between November and April, which is also the hurricane season.

Natural Resources and Marine Life
For the islanders of Oceania, the sea life of the Pacific Ocean is a major source of food and trade. Many people continue to fish and farm in a traditional way, but modern fishing methods have significantly reduced fish stocks, especially tuna.

The seas of Oceania are host to numerous species of fish and to many types of whale, shark and other sea creatures. This is also a region of spectacular coral reefs.

Environment
The Pacific Ocean is currently shrinking because of the movement of the earth's plates. Many of the islands in this region are low-lying, making them particularly vulnerable to rising sea levels. The increasing temperatures across the globe mean that many of the smaller islands in Oceania may disappear within the next few decades.

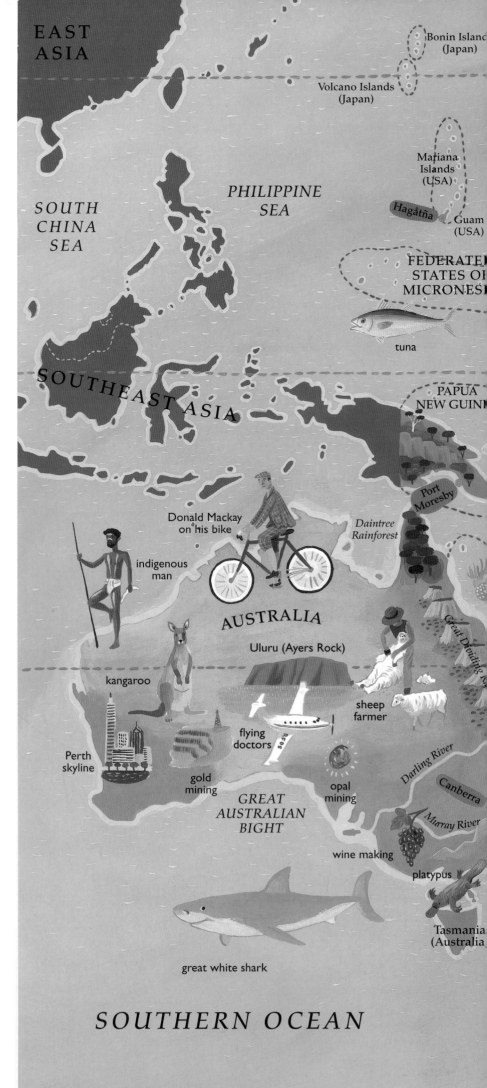

EAST ASIA

Bonin Islands (Japan)

Volcano Islands (Japan)

Mariana Islands (USA)

PHILIPPINE SEA

SOUTH CHINA SEA

Hagåtña

Guam (USA)

FEDERATED STATES OF MICRONESIA

tuna

SOUTHEAST ASIA

PAPUA NEW GUINEA

Port Moresby

Donald Mackay on his bike

Daintree Rainforest

indigenous man

AUSTRALIA

Uluru (Ayers Rock)

Great Dividing Range

kangaroo

sheep farmer

Perth skyline

flying doctors

gold mining

opal mining

GREAT AUSTRALIAN BIGHT

Darling River

Canberra

Murray River

wine making

platypus

Tasmania (Australia)

great white shark

SOUTHERN OCEAN

Tropic of Cancer

Hawaiian Islands (USA)

Polynesian
outrigger

Wake Island
(USA)

surfer

Johnston
Atoll (USA)

Mauna Kea
Observatories

PACIFIC OCEAN

manta ray

MARSHALL
ISLANDS

Palikir

Delap-Uliga-Djarrit

king bird
of paradise

Howland Island (USA)

Line Islands

Equator

Bairiki

Baker Island (USA)

Yaren

NAURU

KIRIBATI

TUVALU

Vaiaku

green
turtle

SOLOMON
ISLANDS

slit
drum

Honiara

rugby

SAMOA

Cook
Islands
(NZ)

CORAL
SEA

VANUATU

Port Vila

Suva

Apia

American
Samoa
(USA)

New
Caledonia
(France)

FIJI

TONGA

Niue
(NZ)

Tahitian dancer

Tropic of Capricorn

horned
parakeet

Nuku'alofa

Coral Sea Islands
(Australia)

French
Polynesia
(France)

Pitcairn
Islands (UK)

Sydney Opera
House

Norfolk
Island
(Australia)

Kermadec
Islands (NZ)

PACIFIC
OCEAN

TASMAN
SEA

Māori
man

International Date Line

kiwi

Wellington

HMS Bounty

Southern Alps

NEW ZEALAND

Chatham
Islands (NZ)

Southeast Asia

Asia is the giant among continents. It's the largest piece of the earth's crust to remain above water, and nearly half the world's population lives in just one part of it: a fertile belt running through south, southeast and east Asia.

Physical Features
Southeast Asia includes the world's largest archipelago, a group of over 17,000 islands sprinkled across the ocean between the Asian mainland and Australia. Four slabs of the earth's crust meet here, so there are numerous volcanoes, and earthquakes are not unusual.

People and Places
The largest country is Indonesia, which has a population nearly half the size of Europe's, scattered across 6,000 islands. Bangkok is the capital and largest city of Thailand with over 6 million people. In contrast, northern Thailand is rural, mountainous and much less densely populated.

Climate and Weather
As the region straddles the equator, the climate is warm and humid. The island of Borneo is home to one of the world's oldest rainforests. The tropical climate is also excellent for growing crops.

Land Use and Natural Resources
Rice is a staple food of the region and is also exported all around the world. Thailand is the world's largest exporter of rice. Rubber is also shipped overseas, as is timber, palm oil, sugarcane, coffee and tin.

Environment
Over 90% of southeast Asia's rainforest has been felled, mostly for timber and to create space for farming. Rainforest canopies absorb carbon dioxide from the atmosphere, so when the trees are felled, carbon is released, contributing to global warming. Today, more and more people are realizing how important it is to preserve the rainforests.

Transport
With so many islands, boats and ships are an important form of transport. The Strait of Malacca is one of the most important shipping lanes in the world, linking the Indian Ocean and the Pacific Ocean.

SOUTH ASIA

Hkakabo Razi

Mt. Popa

BURMA

statue of the Buddha

Ha Nôi

Buddhist monk

LAOS

BAY OF BENGAL

Irrawaddy River

Naypyidaw

Viangchan

VIETNAM

Wat Phra Kaew

Mekong River

paddy fields

tuk-tuk

THAILAND

CAMBODIA

Bangkok

Angkor Wat

Phnum Pénh

GULF OF THAILAND

Sumatran elephant

palm oil plantation

Petronas Towers

Kuala Lumpur

MALAYSIA

Strait of Malacca

Singapore

Sumatran tiger

Sumatra

Malayan tapir

Jakarta

INDIAN OCEAN

EAST ASIA

GULF OF TONKIN

Vietnamese cyclist

SOUTH CHINA SEA

PHILIPPINE SEA

Banaue rice terraces

Luzon

Manila

PHILIPPINES

Palawan

SULU SEA

Sultan's Palace

BRUNEI

Bandar Seri Begawan

orchid

Mt. Kinabalu

CELEBES SEA

Mindanao

jeepney bus

RUBY

PACIFIC OCEAN

Tropic of Cancer

Did You Know?

PALAU

Melekeok

Rajang River

Borneo

Sulawesi

dwarf cuscus

Makassar Strait

red-knobbed hornbill

Halmahera

sulphur-crested cockatoo

Equator

butterflies

orangutan

Buru

Seram

West Papua (Indonesia)

JAVA SEA

coffee plantation

Mt. Semeru

Balinese dancer

INDONESIA

komodo dragon

tree kangaroo

Java

Bali

Lombok

Sumbawa

Flores

Sumba

Dili

EAST TIMOR

West Timor

ARAFURA SEA

Borobodur

TIMOR SEA

East Asia

Everything in east Asia is on a grand scale, from the Great Wall of China to the vast Gobi Desert and the high-altitude Tibetan plateau.

Physical Features

China is an extremely varied land, with mountains, steppes, plateaus and deserts in the west and a vast fertile plain in the east. To the east of China lie the Korean peninsula and the islands of Japan, both of them largely mountainous.

People and Places

At 1.3 billion people, China is the world's most populated country, accounting for one-fifth of the world's population. The Han Chinese, who make up 92% of the population, form the largest single ethnic group in the world. The capital of Japan, Tokyo, is home to 36 million people and is the world's most populous metropolitan area.

Climate and Weather

The countries of east Asia have hot, wet summers and dry, cold winters. Temperatures in the mountainous regions of west China are far cooler than those in the south and east.

Land Use and Natural Resources

Although it has the largest agricultural output in the world, only 15% of China's total land area is cultivated. The main crop here, as in Japan, North and South Korea, is rice. All four countries are major producers of manufactured goods.

Environment

As it changes from a rural to an industrial economy, the way China generates energy is becoming critical to the management of global warming. Around 80% of its electricity comes from coal, but it is exploring more sustainable forms of energy production, including solar power plants in the deserts and offshore wind farms. Japan has been leading the world in pollution reduction since the 1970s with electric trains, a focus on clean, efficient engines and strict anti-pollution laws.

Transport

Japan is one of the most technologically advanced countries in the world and is home to the iconic "Shinkansen", the bullet train which travels at speeds of up to 186mph. As China grows richer, more and more people want to own cars.

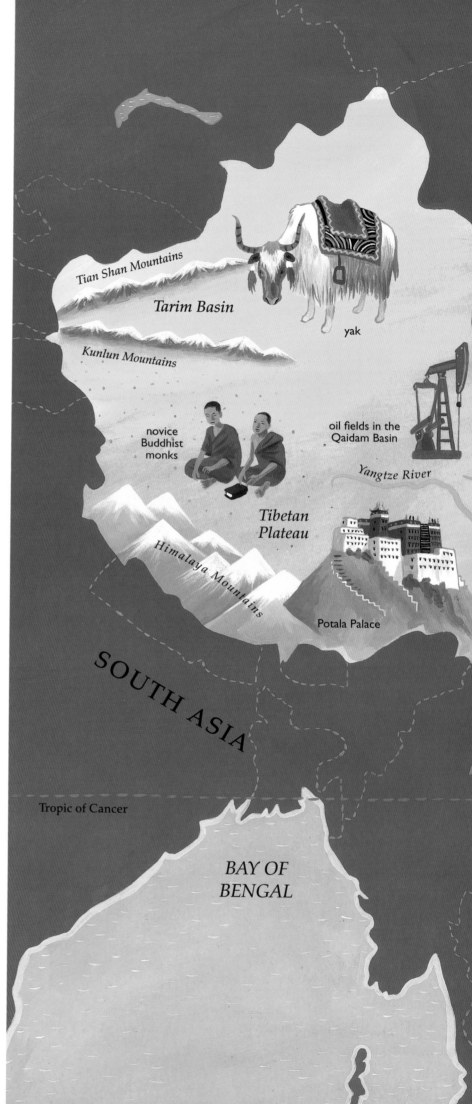

Tian Shan Mountains

Tarim Basin

yak

Kunlun Mountains

novice Buddhist monks

oil fields in the Qaidam Basin

Yangtze River

Tibetan Plateau

Himalaya Mountains

Potala Palace

SOUTH ASIA

Tropic of Cancer

BAY OF BENGAL

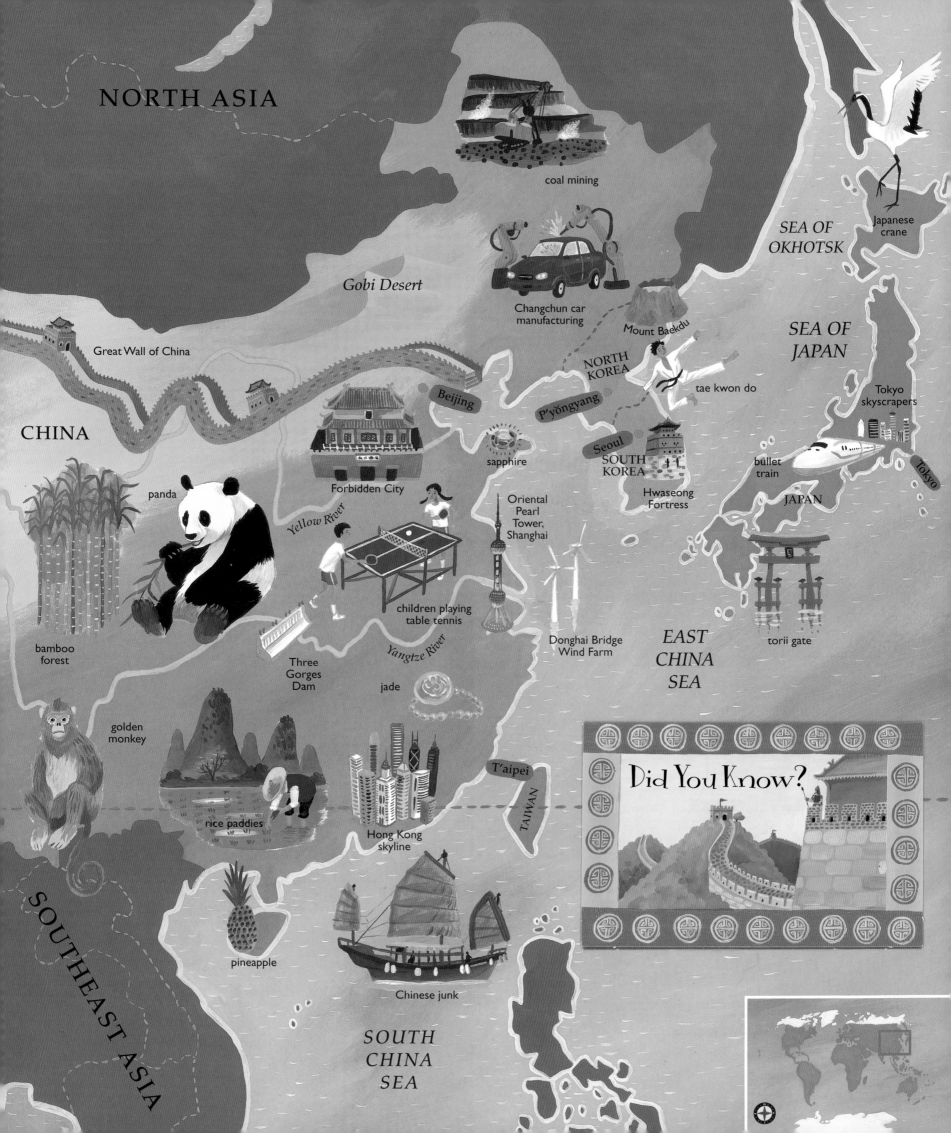

NORTH ASIA

coal mining

Gobi Desert

Changchun car
manufacturing

Mount Baekdu

*SEA OF
OKHOTSK*

Japanese
crane

*SEA OF
JAPAN*

Great Wall of China

NORTH
KOREA

P'yŏngyang

tae kwon do

Tokyo
skyscrapers

CHINA

Beijing

Seoul

SOUTH
KOREA

Hwaseong
Fortress

bullet
train

Tokyo

panda

Forbidden City

sapphire

Oriental
Pearl
Tower,
Shanghai

JAPAN

Yellow River

children playing
table tennis

bamboo
forest

Three
Gorges
Dam

Yangtze River

jade

Donghai Bridge
Wind Farm

torii gate

*EAST
CHINA
SEA*

golden
monkey

rice paddies

Hong Kong
skyline

T'aipei

TAIWAN

Did You Know?

pineapple

Chinese junk

SOUTHEAST ASIA

*SOUTH
CHINA
SEA*

North Asia

North Asia includes the world's largest country, the Russian Federation, and one of the world's remotest landscapes, the Gobi Desert.

Physical Features

This region is home to some of the harshest environments on Earth, including wide expanses of frozen tundra, deserts that stretch across Mongolia and the high, remote volcanoes of the Kamchatka peninsula in eastern Siberia.

People and Places

Although nearly twice the size of the United States, the Russian Federation only has half its population. Moscow is the region's most populous city with over 10 million inhabitants. At the other extreme, many people in the Arctic regions remain seminomadic, tending large reindeer herds which provide much of their food and wealth.

Climate and Weather

Because the Russian Federation extends so far north, the climate can be harsh. In winter, temperatures in Siberia, a region east of the Ural Mountains, can fall to –76°F. The town of Oymyakon claims to be the coldest inhabited place on Earth.

Land Use and Natural Resources

Due to the harsh climate and landscape, less than one-tenth of Russia is cultivated. Most people live west of the Ural Mountains on a vast, fertile plain used for growing cereals like wheat and barley. The Russian Federation is the planet's fossil-fuel giant. It has the world's largest natural gas reserves, the second-largest coal reserves and the eighth-largest oil reserves. Russia has so much fossil fuel that 55% of its energy comes from natural gas, and only 5% from nuclear.

Wildlife

The Russian Federation is a sanctuary for some of the rarest animals on the planet, including the snow crane and the Siberian tiger.

Transport

The majority of Russian personal and cargo transport is by train, as the road system is not extensive and often in disrepair. There are many urban rapid-transit systems as well as the Trans-Siberian Railway, which has 5,592 miles of track.

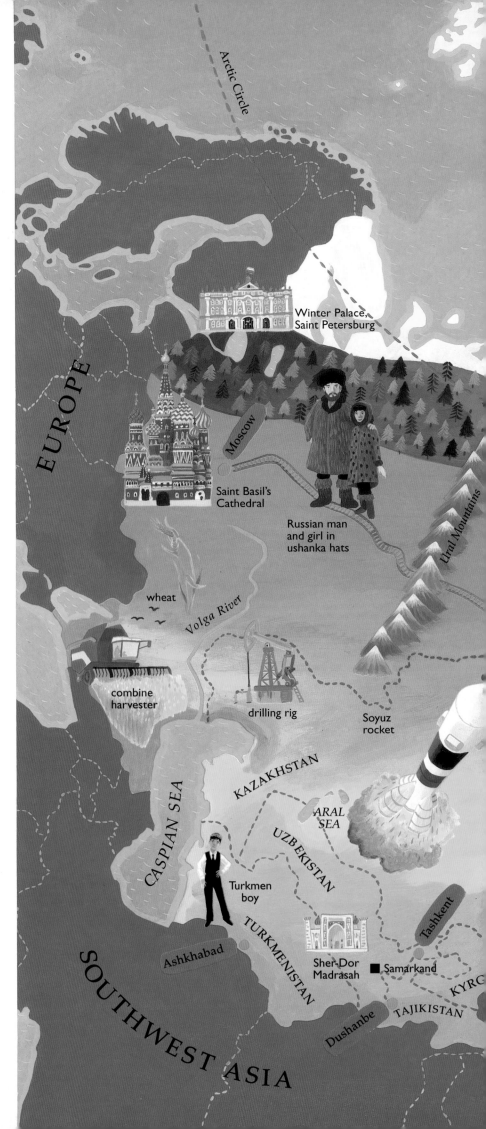

Arctic Circle

Winter Palace, Saint Petersburg

EUROPE

Moscow

Saint Basil's Cathedral

Russian man and girl in ushanka hats

Ural Mountains

wheat

Volga River

combine harvester

drilling rig

Soyuz rocket

KAZAKHSTAN

CASPIAN SEA

ARAL SEA

UZBEKISTAN

Turkmen boy

TURKMENISTAN

Tashkent

Ashkhabad

Sher-Dor Madrasah

Samarkand

KYR

Dushanbe

TAJIKISTAN

SOUTHWEST ASIA

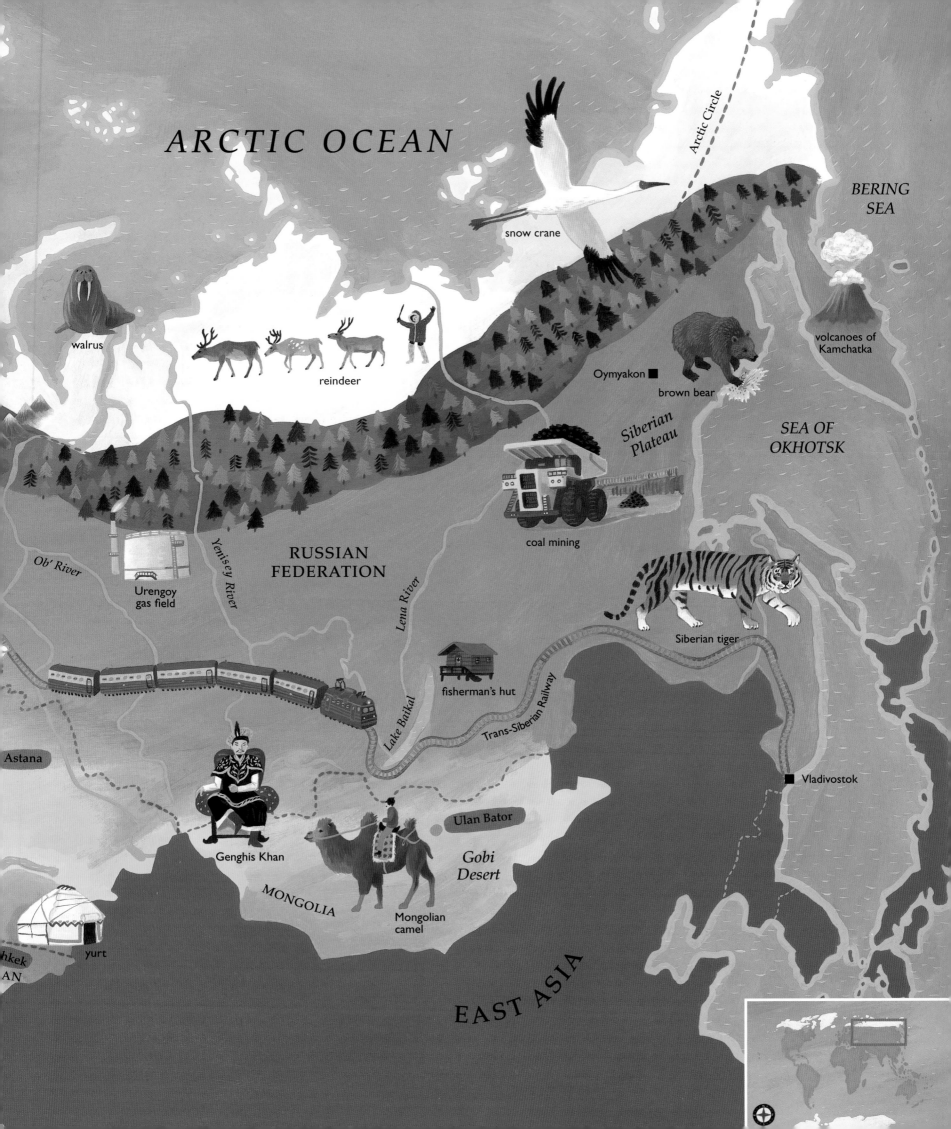

ARCTIC OCEAN

BERING SEA

snow crane

walrus

reindeer

Oymyakon ■

brown bear

Siberian Plateau

SEA OF OKHOTSK

volcanoes of Kamchatka

coal mining

Ob' River

Yemisey River

RUSSIAN FEDERATION

Lena River

Urengoy gas field

Siberian tiger

fisherman's hut

Trans-Siberian Railway

Lake Baikal

Astana

Vladivostok

Genghis Khan

Ulan Bator

Gobi Desert

MONGOLIA

Mongolian camel

hkek
AN

yurt

EAST ASIA

South Asia

This is one of the most heavily populated parts of Asia. Its landscapes range from low, fertile plains to the heights of the Himalayan peaks.

Physical Features
Around 70 million years ago, this section of the earth's crust collided with east Asia, pushing up folds of rock to form the Himalayas. Among them is Mount Everest, the highest mountain in the world at 29,029ft. In 1953, Edmund Hillary and Tenzing Norgay made the first successful ascent of Mount Everest.

People and Places
Three-quarters of a billion people in this region rely on river water that comes from melting ice and snow in the mountains. India is the largest country in the region, and the second-most-populous country in the world, after China.

Climate and Weather
Southern parts of south Asia have hot summers and monsoon rains, while the Himalayas are snowcapped all year round. Pakistan experiences some of the most extreme temperatures on Earth, ranging from 122°F in the south in summer to -58°F in the northern mountain ranges in winter.

Land Use and Natural Resources
Afghanistan is largely mountainous, with just 15% of the land suitable for farming. At the mouth of the Brahmaputra and Ganges rivers is Bangladesh, where the soil and climate are so favorable for agriculture that farmers often harvest three crops a year.

Environment
The average Indian is very "green," emitting just 1 ton of carbon dioxide per year through burning fossil fuels, compared to 20 tons per year for the average American and 88 tons for a person living in Qatar.

Wildlife
This region is home to many rare species, among them the Bengal tiger, the Asiatic lion, the snow leopard, the one-horned rhinoceros and the Indian elephant. The Indian elephant is a subspecies of the Asian elephant and is the largest land animal in Asia.

NORTH ASIA

Hindu Kush Mountains

woman in burqa Kabul

Friday Mosque

Helmand River

AFGHANISTAN

SOUTHWEST ASIA

pomegranate farm

PAKISTAN

sacred fig tree

water buffalo and egret

GULF OF OMAN

sacred cow

fishing boat

ARABIAN SEA

Did You Know?

EAST ASIA

Karakoram Mountains

snow leopard

Islamabad

Golden Temple

Lahore Fort

Indus River

Thar Desert

New Delhi

woman carrying water

Mehrangarh Fort

Taj Mahal

blue houses of Jodhpur

INDIA

Himalaya Mountains

NEPAL

Mt. Everest

Edmund Hillary

Thimphu

BHUTAN

Kathmandu

bathers in the Ganges

Ganges River

Brahmaputra River

Bengal tiger

INDIA

tea pickers

Tropic of Cancer

boy playing cricket

Dhaka

BANGLADESH

SOUTHEAST ASIA

Satpura Range

Bombay stock exchange

General Post Office, Kolkata

BAY OF BENGAL

Deccan Plateau

Indian peacock

Gateway of India

Ambassador car

tuk-tuk

banyan tree

Andaman Islands (India)

Lakshadweep (India)

Kapaleeshwarar Temple

Indian elephant

Sri Lankan girl

Nicobar Islands (India)

Sri Lankan stilt fisherman

SRI LANKA

Sri Jayewardenepura Kotte

INDIAN OCEAN

Malé

THE MALDIVES

Southwest Asia

Southwest Asia (also known as the "Middle East") lies at a continental crossroads between Asia, Europe and Africa.

Physical Features

Most of this region is desert, yet within it are the snowcapped Caucasus and Elborz mountains, and the world's largest body of enclosed water, the Caspian Sea. The Rub' al Khali is the world's largest expanse of sand.

People and Places

The world's first civilization took root in what is now Iraq in the sixth millennium BCE. Between the Tigris and Euphrates Rivers, the Sumerian people built great cities surrounded by fields and orchards. Much of Iran is a vast plateau over 3,281ft high and ringed with mountains. Tehran is the largest city in southwest Asia, with a population of 15 million.

Climate and Weather

Most of southwest Asia is either arid or semiarid, so drought is an increasing challenge. Temperatures in Saudi Arabia can reach up to 129°F in summer. At the other extreme, the summit of Mount Damavand, the highest peak in Iran at 18,606ft, remains snowcapped all year round.

Land Use and Natural Resources

Saudi Arabia is by far the biggest country in the region and has one-fifth of the world's oil reserves. Combined with Iran, Qatar and the United Arab Emirates (UAE), the region has the greatest proven reserves of natural gas in the world after the Russian Federation.

Environment

Some of the world's most astonishing cities are found in southwest Asia, such as Dubai, which is home to the Burj Al Arab, the fourth-tallest hotel in the world. Carbon emissions in parts of southwest Asia are by far the highest in the world — a person in the UAE on average emits 15 times more than a person in China.

Wildlife

Species found in southwest Asia include cheetahs, lynx, lizards, turtles, whales and dolphins. The rarest bird in the region is the northern bald ibis, which is critically endangered, but some have recently been discovered in Syria.

BLACK SEA

EUROPE

Blue Mosque

Library of Celsus

apricots

Ankara

TURKEY

northern bald ibis

SYRIA

Nicosia

MEDITERRANEAN SEA

CYPRUS

Roman ruins at Palmyra

Beirut

LEBANON

Damascus

Jerusalem

ISRAEL

'Amman

DEAD SEA

JORDAN

Cypriot Navy patrol boat

GULF OF SUEZ

RED SEA

NORTH AFRICA

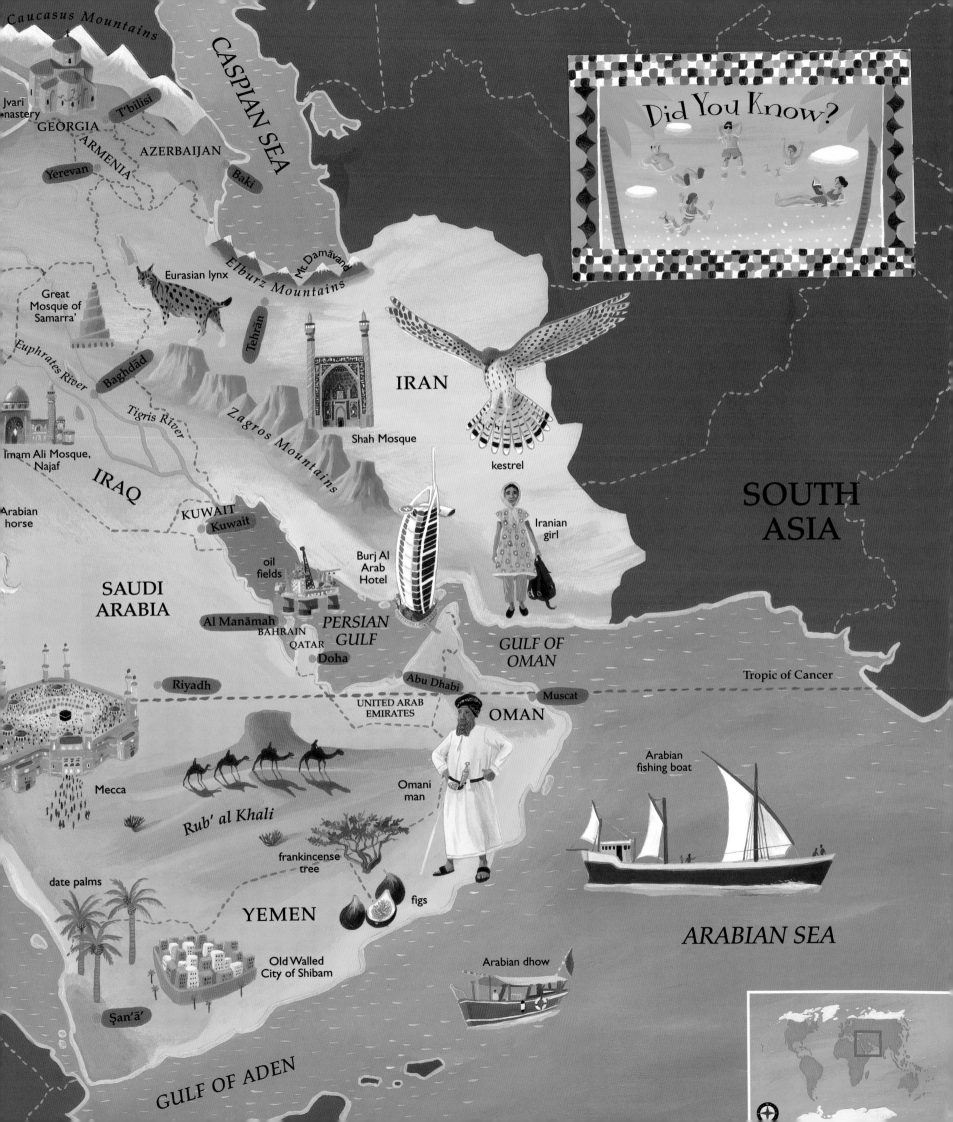

Caucasus Mountains

CASPIAN SEA

Jvari
nastery

T'bilisi

GEORGIA

ARMENIA

AZERBAIJAN

Yerevan

Baki

Great
Mosque of
Samarra'

Eurasian lynx

Elburz Mountains

Mt. Damāvand

Euphrates River

Baghdād

Tehrān

IRAN

Tigris River

Zagros Mountains

Ímam Ali Mosque,
Najaf

Shah Mosque

kestrel

IRAQ

Arabian
horse

KUWAIT

Kuwait

Iranian
girl

**SOUTH
ASIA**

oil
fields

**SAUDI
ARABIA**

Burj Al
Arab
Hotel

Al Manāmah

BAHRAIN

QATAR

**PERSIAN
GULF**

Doha

*GULF OF
OMAN*

Riyadh

Abu Dhabi

Muscat

Tropic of Cancer

**UNITED ARAB
EMIRATES**

OMAN

Omani
man

Arabian
fishing boat

Mecca

Rub' al Khali

frankincense
tree

figs

date palms

ARABIAN SEA

YEMEN

Old Walled
City of Shibam

Arabian dhow

Şan'ā'

GULF OF ADEN

Did You Know?

Europe

The second-smallest continent on the planet is an intricate jigsaw of 43 countries inhabited by 580 million people who speak 35 different languages.

Physical Features
With its many peninsulas and seas, Europe has an extraordinarily long coastline, which varies in character from deep Norwegian fjords to the sandy beaches of Greece and great river deltas like the Danube. Inland, there are many mountain ranges, including the Alps and Carpathians, which together stretch for 1,243 miles across the heart of the continent. About 25% of the land area of the Netherlands is below sea level, so has to be protected from flooding.

People and Places
About 75% of Europeans live in or around cities, which often sprawl out into smaller suburbs. Some geographers call the crescent of cities, towns, suburbs and industrial areas stretching from south to north across Europe the Blue Banana, a megalopolis of one hundred and ten million people. Several countries in Europe are so small that they cannot even feature on a map of this scale, such as Andorra, Liechtenstein, Monaco and San Marino.

Climate and Weather
Europe has a wide range of climates because its northern edge reaches far beyond the Arctic Circle while its southern boundary almost touches Africa. Northern Scandinavia has an alpine tundra climate and temperatures in Iceland have reached a record low of −36.2°F, though the Gulf Stream warms it considerably. This Atlantic current also affects the rest of Europe, making it generally warmer than other regions at this latitude. Southern Europe's Mediterranean climate is one of warm, dry summers and mild, wet winters.

Land Use and Natural Resources
Much of Europe is richly fertile and has historically been excellent for the cultivation of crops. These range from olive groves in the Mediterranean south to more frost-tolerant cereals and pulses in central and northern countries. France is well known for its fields of lavender. Some parts of the region are also rich in coal.

Environment
It was Europeans who drove the change from making things by hand to making them with machines. Known as the Industrial Revolution, this "machine age" marked the start of a sudden increase in fossil fuel emissions, which contribute to global warming. Europeans are now trying to decrease their harmful emissions. Germany has taken the lead in developing solar power. Austria and Sweden generate about half of their electricity from hydropower. Denmark produces a higher proportion of its electricity from wind power than any other country and manufactures around half of all wind turbines worldwide.

Did You Know?

Wildlife
Animals such as reindeer and moose live in the Arctic north, while in the Mediterranean south there are heat-loving animals including snakes and scorpions. Wild boars, also known as wild pigs, inhabit much of northern and central Europe. If caught unawares, they can be quite aggressive in their behavior.

Transport
Europe is one of the easiest regions to travel around, as most places are accessible by rail, road, air or sea. Steam-powered rail transport originated in England in the 1800s and the rail network has now expanded to include the entire European continent. The Channel Tunnel runs under the English Channel and connects the United Kingdom to the rest of Europe's rail system. Europe also has some of the world's busiest airports and seaports.

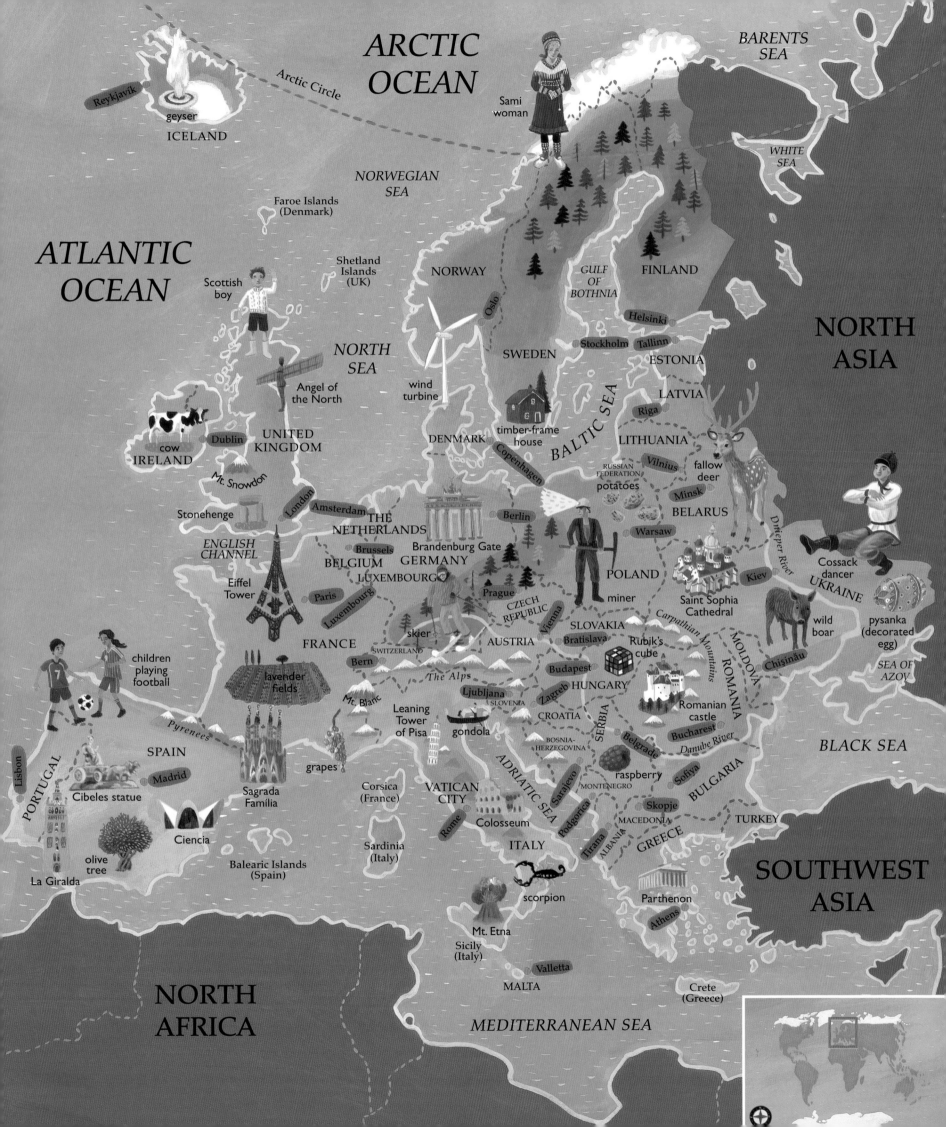

ARCTIC OCEAN

BARENTS SEA

Arctic Circle

Reykjavik
geyser
ICELAND

Sami woman

WHITE SEA

ATLANTIC OCEAN

NORWEGIAN SEA

NORTH ASIA

Faroe Islands (Denmark)

Shetland Islands (UK)

NORWAY

SWEDEN

GULF OF BOTHNIA

FINLAND

Scottish boy

Oslo

Helsinki

NORTH SEA

wind turbine

Stockholm
Tallinn
ESTONIA

Angel of the North

BALTIC SEA

LATVIA

Riga

cow
IRELAND

Dublin

UNITED KINGDOM

DENMARK

timber-frame house

Copenhagen

LITHUANIA

Vilnius
fallow deer

Mt. Snowdon

RUSSIAN FEDERATION

Minsk
BELARUS

potatoes

Stonehenge

London

Amsterdam

THE NETHERLANDS

Berlin

Warsaw

ENGLISH CHANNEL

Brussels

BELGIUM

Brandenburg Gate

GERMANY

Dnieper River

Eiffel Tower

LUXEMBOURG

Saint Sophia Cathedral

Kiev

Cossack dancer

UKRAINE

Paris

Luxembourg

Prague

CZECH REPUBLIC

miner

POLAND

pysanka (decorated egg)

FRANCE

children playing football

lavender fields

Bern
SWITZERLAND

skier

Vienna

AUSTRIA

SLOVAKIA

Bratislava

Carpathian Mountains

wild boar

Rubik's cube

MOLDOVA

Chişinău

SEA OF AZOV

Mt. Blanc

The Alps

Budapest

HUNGARY

Zagreb

SLOVENIA

Ljubljana

ROMANIA

Romanian castle

Bucharest

Pyrenees

grapes

Leaning Tower of Pisa

gondola

CROATIA

SERBIA

Belgrade

Danube River

BLACK SEA

SPAIN

Lisbon

Madrid

Cibeles statue

Ciencia

PORTUGAL

olive tree

La Giralda

Sagrada Família

Corsica (France)

VATICAN CITY

Colosseum

ITALY

ADRIATIC SEA

BOSNIA-HERZEGOVINA

Sarajevo

MONTENEGRO

Podgorica

raspberry

Sofiya

BULGARIA

Skopje

MACEDONIA

Tirana

ALBANIA

GREECE

TURKEY

Sardinia (Italy)

Balearic Islands (Spain)

scorpion

Parthenon

Athens

SOUTHWEST ASIA

Mt. Etna

Sicily (Italy)

Valletta

MALTA

Crete (Greece)

NORTH AFRICA

MEDITERRANEAN SEA

North Africa

Africa is the second-largest continent in the world, with over 50 countries, a population of about one billion and around 2,000 languages.

Physical Features

The Sahara is the largest desert on Earth, covering over 5.6 million square miles. It is expanding southwards at an average of half a mile per month. The desert is not all sand, but includes gravel plains, salt flats and mountains.

People and Places

Most of the people in north Africa live near the coasts or on the banks of rivers. In Egypt, 90% of the population lives on the banks of the Nile River and on its enormous delta.

Cairo is the largest city in Africa, with a population of 18 million. By comparison, only 2 million people inhabit the Sahara Desert. The newest country is South Sudan, declaring its independence on July 9, 2011.

Climate and Weather

North Africa has the hottest place in the world: The highest temperature ever recorded was 136°F in El Azizia, Libya in 1922. Half of the Sahara receives less than an inch of rain per year, whereas some of the highest of the Tibesti Mountains receive as much as 4.7in annually.

Land Use and Natural Resources

Historically, the countries of north Africa have followed small-scale farming methods. Much of the land has been depleted by war and by overcultivation from occupying powers. Some countries, like Algeria, Libya and Nigeria, have large oil reserves.

Environment

Africa is the continent that is most vulnerable to the impacts of climate change as it will get even hotter due to global warming. However, the average African burns far less fossil fuel than most people on the planet.

Transport

The Nile River has been used as a transport route for people and goods for over 2,000 years. The Trans-Sahara Highway, from Algiers to Lagos, is one of the oldest and most complete transnational highways in Africa.

EUROPE

Berber goat herd

Algiers

Tunis

Tunisian boy

Tripoli

Mountains

cobra

TUNISIA

El Azizia

ALGERIA

Leptis Magna
(Roman ruins)

Sahara Desert

LIBYA

Ahaggar Mountains

Tibesti Mountains

Emi Koussi

NIGER

nomad

black crowned crane

Niger River

baobab tree

CHAD

lady going to market

Niamey

Lake Chad

Ouagadougou

Nduamena

bus

Abuja

snail

TOGO

BENIN

NIGERIA

Lagos

CAMEROON

Chad-Cameroon oil pipeline

CENTRAL AFRICAN REPUBLIC

oil well

Lomé

Porto-Novo

Accra

Yaoundé

Bangui

BLACK
SEA

CASPIAN SEA

MEDITERRANEAN SEA

SOUTHWEST ASIA

Cairo skyline

Suez Canal

Cairo

PERSIAN GULF

pyramids

ancient
Egyptian
man

Tropic of Cancer

dates

EGYPT

RED SEA

felucca
boat

scorpion

Jebel Barkal

Nile River

Sudanese
children

gazelle

Asmara

Blue Nile

ERITREA

Burj
Al-Fateh
Hotel

Khartoum

White Nile

Djibouti

GULF OF ADEN

martial
eagle

The Church
of Saint George

DJIBOUTI

Arabian dhow

SUDAN

baboon

Nile crocodile

ETHIOPIA

SOMALIA

Āddīs Ābeba

African wild dog

Ethiopian Highlands

SOUTH
SUDAN

Juba

SOUTHERN
AFRICA

Mogadishu

Southern Africa

Southern Africa is a region of extraordinary contrasts and great cultural diversity. It is considered to be the birthplace of man.

Physical Features
The landscapes of Southern Africa range from rainforests, immense rivers and spiky mountain ranges to fertile farmland and deserts. At 19,341ft, the highest mountain on the continent is Mount Kilimanjaro in Tanzania.

People and Places
At the tip of the continent is South Africa, the wealthiest country in the region. Cape Town, the legislative capital of South Africa, is overlooked by Table Mountain. The indigenous people of the Kalahari Desert, the San Bushmen, speak a unique "click" language.

Climate and Weather
The varied climate of southern Africa includes arid, hot deserts and wet, lush rainforests. In contrast, there are still glaciers at the summit of Mount Kilimanjaro, though scientists have predicted that these will have melted by 2020.

Land Use and Natural Resources
Countries in the east of the region were the first to domesticate coffee, sorghum and watermelon. In the west, staple crops include yams and rice. The Congo Basin provides fresh water, food and shelter to 75 million people, but it is under threat from logging, hunting, farming and mining. The rest of the world needs the Congo Basin too, because its vast rainforest soaks up carbon dioxide.

Environment
The region's biggest consumer of energy is South Africa, which has a lot of sunshine but no oil reserves. To help fulfill their energy needs, many South Africans use solar water heaters. Solar-powered traffic lights have been installed at some Cape Town road intersections. South Africa also has about 280,000 windmills, second only to Australia.

Wildlife
The Congo Basin is the world's second-largest tropical rainforest and is home to many species, from mountain gorillas to rare butterflies. In Tanzania, the Serengeti boasts the largest seasonal migration of nearly 2 million herbivores.

Malabo

EQUATORIAL GUINEA

SÃO TOMÉ AND PRÍNCIPE   São Tomé

Libreville

GABON

CONGO

Brazzaville

Kinshasa

Cabinda Province (Angola)

National Bank of Angola

Luanda

ATLANTIC OCEAN

guinea fowl

Namib Desert

Did You Know?

swallow

NORTH AFRICA

INDIAN OCEAN

Equator

gorilla

Congo Basin

Congo River

De Brazza's monkey

UGANDA

Great Rift Valley

Samburu warrior

KENYA

Kampala

Lake Victoria

tea picking

Mt. Kenya

Nairobi

RWANDA
Kigali

Mt. Kilimanjaro

Riyadha Mosque

DEMOCRATIC REPUBLIC OF CONGO

okapi

Bujumbura

BURUNDI

Serengeti

TANZANIA

Dodoma

Pemba

Zanzibar

Victoria

SEYCHELLES

woman carrying water

diamonds

Stanley and Livingstone

giraffe

safari vehicle

fishing boat

COMOROS

Moroni

tomato frog

ANGOLA

zebra

MALAWI

Lake Malawi

ring-tailed lemur

ZAMBIA

lion

Lusaka

Lilongwe

cichlid fish

San bushmen

Zambezi River

Harare

hippopotamus

Catholic church

MOZAMBIQUE

MOZAMBIQUE CHANNEL

Antananarivo

MAURITIUS

Port Louis

NAMIBIA

BOTSWANA

Victoria Falls

ZIMBABWE

MADAGASCAR

Réunion (France)

Kalahari Desert

Limpopo River

rice terraces

Tropic of Capricorn

African elephant

coconut

Gaborone

Maputo

rugby players

gold

Mbabane

SWAZILAND

SOUTH AFRICA

LESOTHO

Maseru

Cape Town skyscrapers

Cape Town

North America

The Americas are named after the Italian explorer Amerigo Vespucci, although Christopher Columbus and John Cabot are often credited as the first European "discoverers." This region is a melting pot of nationalities despite being made up of only two countries, Canada and the USA.

Physical Features

North America has a spectacular variety of physical features, from forests, grasslands and deserts to glaciers and mountains. The Rocky Mountains stretch 2,983 miles from British Columbia in Canada to New Mexico in the USA. The longest river on the continent, the Mississippi-Missouri, starts in the Rockies and flows for 3,709 miles to the Gulf of Mexico. In between lies a huge swath of flat grassland, steppe and prairie that makes up the Great Plains of the Midwest.

People and Places

The largest country in North America is Canada. It is also the second-largest country in the world, yet it has less than 1% of the world's population.

For centuries, North America was inhabited by a wide variety of native peoples. From the early 18th century, the slave trade forcibly brought millions of African peoples here. Then, between 1820 and 1910, many millions of immigrants, most of them from Europe, settled in the USA and Canada. Much of Quebec, in eastern Canada, was settled by French colonists and it remains a largely French-speaking province.

Climate and Weather

North America has many different climatic zones, from the cold Arctic coast to the hot and sunny south. The east coast of the United States is relatively mild and humid; the west coast has a warmer, drier climate. Canada is cooler, with a polar climate above the Arctic Circle.

The region experiences some very destructive weather, including hurricanes on the Atlantic and Gulf coasts, damaging wind cyclones in the Midwest's Tornado Alley and devastating wildfires in the west coast's dry climate.

NORTH ASIA

ARCTIC OCEAN

BERING SEA

BERING STRAIT

iceberg

BEAUFORT SEA

Brooks Range

truck

Yukon River

Trans-Alaska Pipeline

brown bear

Our Lady of Victory Church

salmon

Alaska (USA)

GULF OF ALASKA

Rocky Mountains

Queen Charlotte Islands

PACIFIC OCEAN

Vancouver Island

totem pole

bald eagle

turquoise jewellery

Golden Gate Bridge

Grand Canyon

Los Angeles skyline

Colorado River

cactu

Queen Elizabeth
Islands

gyrfalcon

BAFFIN BAY

Inuit
kayaker

muskox

Victoria
Island

purple saxifrage

Baffin Island

DAVIS STRAIT

Arctic
hare

harp
seal

Canada
goose

ice
hockey
player

buffalo

HUDSON
BAY

logging

CANADA

moose

Belcher
Islands

Newfoundland

Anticosti
Island

mounted
policeman

grain elevator

maple
tree

Château
Frontenac

Prince
Edward
Island

lobster

Missouri River

durum
wheat

The Great
Lakes

CN
Tower

Ottawa

Niagara
Falls

ATLANTIC
OCEAN

UNITED
STATES OF
AMERICA

cherries

Statue of
Liberty

Mount
Rushmore

the White
House

Washington DC

American
football
player

Mississippi River

cotton

space
shuttle

oil
fields

peanuts

Rio Grande River

paddle steamer

alligator

MEXICO,
CENTRAL AMERICA
AND THE CARIBBEAN

GULF OF
MEXICO

Arctic Circle

Mexico, Central America and the Caribbean

Though these countries are part of the North American continent, their culture is very distinct from the USA and Canada.

Physical Features
Stretching south from the USA into the tropics, Central America is a tapering tail of land forming a narrow bridge into South America. Facing it across the Caribbean Sea is an arc of 7,000 or so islands, islets and reefs. The region sits on the junction of several of the earth's crustal plates, forming several mountain ranges and volcanoes. The Panama Canal is a 48-mile ship canal joining the Atlantic and Pacific Oceans, replacing the long and treacherous route around the tip of South America.

People and Places
Central America's ethnic character can be traced back to the mixing of the European conquistadors and the indigenous peoples. Over half of the 190 million people in this region live in Mexico, with an astonishing 20 million gathered in the greater part of Mexico City, which is the largest city in the region. Belize is the only country in this area with English as its official language.

Climate and Weather
The weather can vary between extremes with wet weather from June to October and dry weather from November to May.

Land Use and Natural Resources
The landscape ranges from arid desert to lush rainforest. Most of the economy is based on agriculture, with maize, wheat and rice being the main cereal crops. On the mainland there are many cattle ranches, providing beef for export. The biggest Caribbean island, Cuba, is the world's third-largest producer of sugar.

Environment
Cubans generate electricity by burning the leftovers from sugarcane factories. In the capital, Havana, thousands of Cubans grow organic vegetables in tiny urban plots known as *organopónicos*. Mexico has one of the largest geothermal power-producing areas in the world, which supplies energy to the United States and Belize.

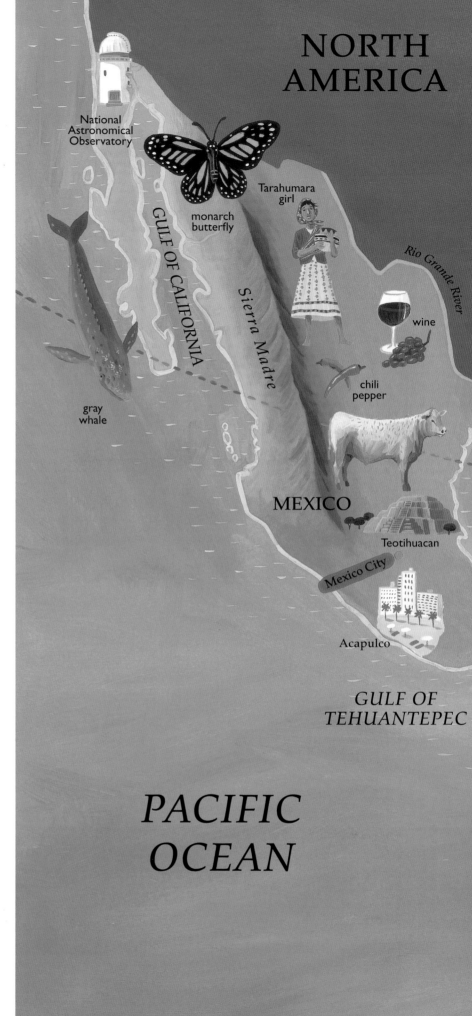

NORTH AMERICA

National Astronomical Observatory

monarch butterfly

Tarahumara girl

GULF OF CALIFORNIA

Sierra Madre

Rio Grande River

wine

chili pepper

gray whale

MEXICO

Teotihuacan

Mexico City

Acapulco

GULF OF TEHUANTEPEC

PACIFIC OCEAN

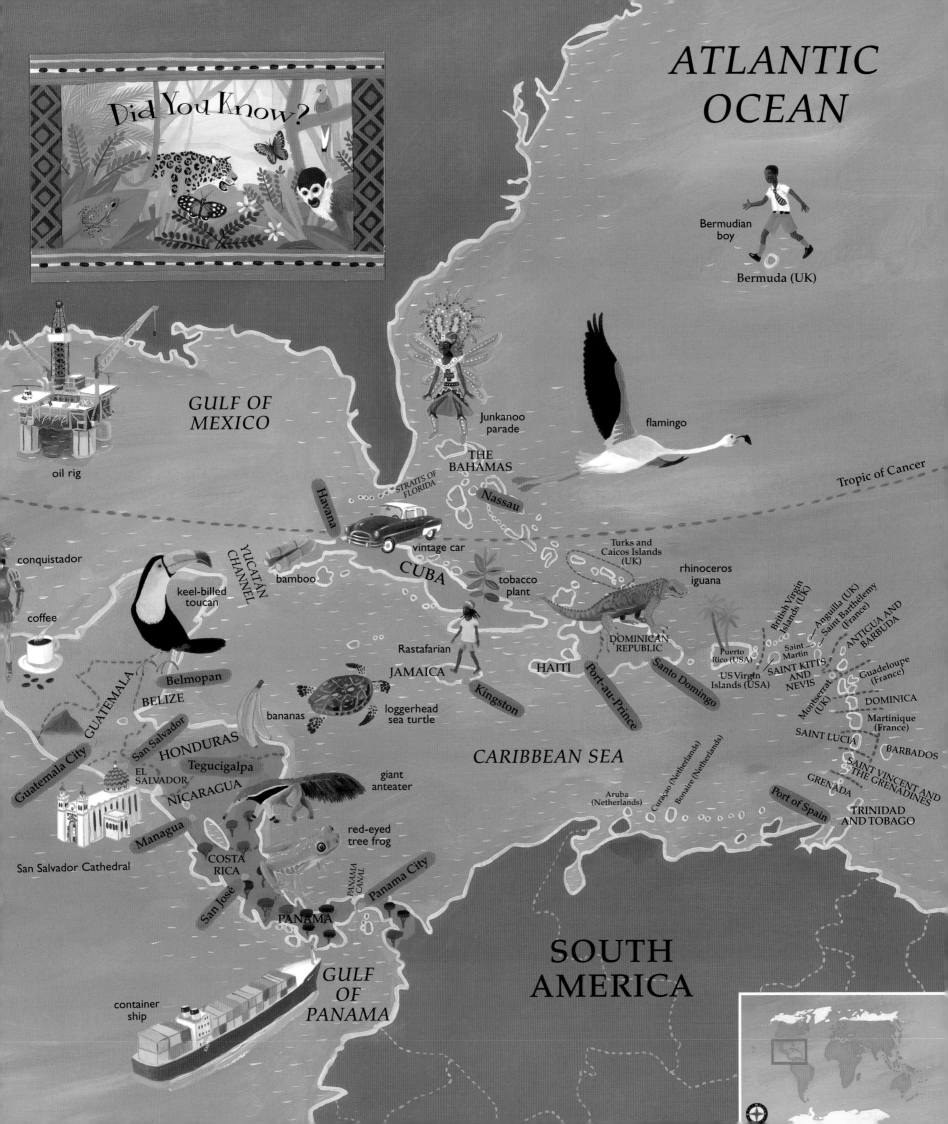

ATLANTIC OCEAN

Did You Know?

GULF OF MEXICO

oil rig

Bermudian boy

Bermuda (UK)

Junkanoo parade

flamingo

Tropic of Cancer

THE BAHAMAS

STRAITS OF FLORIDA

Nassau

Havana

vintage car

CUBA

conquistador

YUCATÁN CHANNEL

keel-billed toucan

bamboo

coffee

tobacco plant

Turks and Caicos Islands (UK)

rhinoceros iguana

DOMINICAN REPUBLIC

HAITI

Port-au-Prince

Santo Domingo

British Virgin Islands (UK)

Anguilla (UK)

Saint Barthelemy (France)

Puerto Rico (USA)

Saint Martin

ANTIGUA AND BARBUDA

US Virgin Islands (USA)

SAINT KITTS AND NEVIS

Montserrat (UK)

Guadeloupe (France)

DOMINICA

Martinique (France)

Rastafarian

JAMAICA

Kingston

GUATEMALA

Belmopan

BELIZE

bananas

loggerhead sea turtle

SAINT LUCIA

BARBADOS

CARIBBEAN SEA

Guatemala City

San Salvador

HONDURAS

Tegucigalpa

EL SALVADOR

NICARAGUA

giant anteater

SAINT VINCENT AND THE GRENADINES

Curaçao (Netherlands)

Bonaire (Netherlands)

GRENADA

Port of Spain

Aruba (Netherlands)

TRINIDAD AND TOBAGO

Managua

San Salvador Cathedral

COSTA RICA

red-eyed tree frog

PANAMA CANAL

Panama City

San José

PANAMA

SOUTH AMERICA

container ship

GULF OF PANAMA

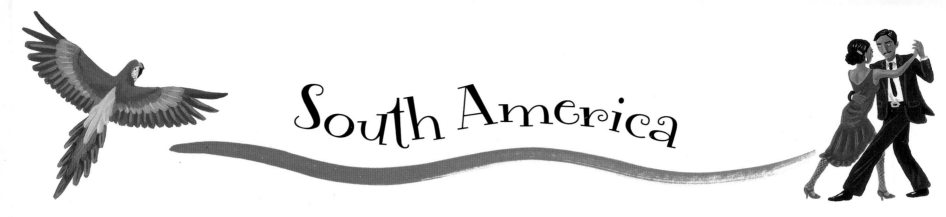

South America

Nowhere else in the world do so many humans coexist with such an important natural habitat. South America is home to 374 million people and to over one-third of the world's species of land-based plants and animals.

Physical Features

The Amazon Rainforest is the largest surviving tropical rainforest on the planet, and has been evolving over millions of years. It takes its name from the longest river on the continent, the Amazon, which is also considered by some to be the longest river in the world. The western side of the continent is dominated by the Andes, the longest mountain range in the world. The highest peak is Aconcagua at 22,831ft, which has a number of glaciers. It is the highest mountain outside Asia.

People and Places

The population of South America is a combination of native peoples, settlers from southern Europe — largely Portugal and Spain — and people of African descent, who came to the continent in the eighteenth century. In the Amazon region, there are 60–90 tribes who have had no contact with the outside world. There are only about 100 uncontacted tribes worldwide. Today, over three-quarters of South Americans live in towns and cities. São Paulo, in Brazil, has more inhabitants than New York City and is the most populous city in the Americas.

Climate and Weather

West of the Andes, the climate shows dramatic contrasts — the Atacama Desert in Chile is the driest in the world whereas northern Colombia is one of the wettest regions in the world. Northeast of the Andes, much of the continent's climate is tropical, but southeast of the mountain range, the climate is much cooler and often windy.

Land Use and Natural Resources

The fertile pampas, or grasslands, of Argentina are used to rear beef cattle and cultivate wheat. Cattle are also raised in northern Colombia and Venezuela. In Brazil, coffee is a major crop, and so is sugarcane, which is converted to biofuel. Brazil is also the largest producer and consumer of sugar in the world.

South America is rich in fossil fuels. Colombia has vast coal reserves, while Venezuela's oil makes it the richest country in the region. Flowing northwest in the Pacific from southern Chile to northern Peru, the Humboldt Current has helped to create the most abundant marine ecosystem in the world, as well as the world's largest fisheries, including anchovies and sardines.

Did You Know?

Environment

The Amazon Rainforest accounts for over half of the world's remaining rainforest and covers 1.4 billion acres. The size of the rainforest is being reduced due to logging and farming. In addition to the staggering loss of plant life this clearing of the rainforest causes, many animal species are declining due to habitat loss. The rainforest is also sensitive to climate change. Scientists predict that if the earth's global temperature increases by 7°F, up to 85% of the rainforest could be lost.

Wildlife

One in ten of all known species and one in five of all bird species are found in the Amazon Rainforest. Around 3,000 species of freshwater fauna have been found in Amazonia and scientists think there may be as many as 6,000 more species waiting to be discovered. Among the many other varied species of the Amazon are over 1,000 types of frogs, including the poison dart frog. Of the 1,500 species of birds found in the Amazon Rainforest, the red-and-green macaw is one of the most striking, but its numbers are declining due to loss of habitat.

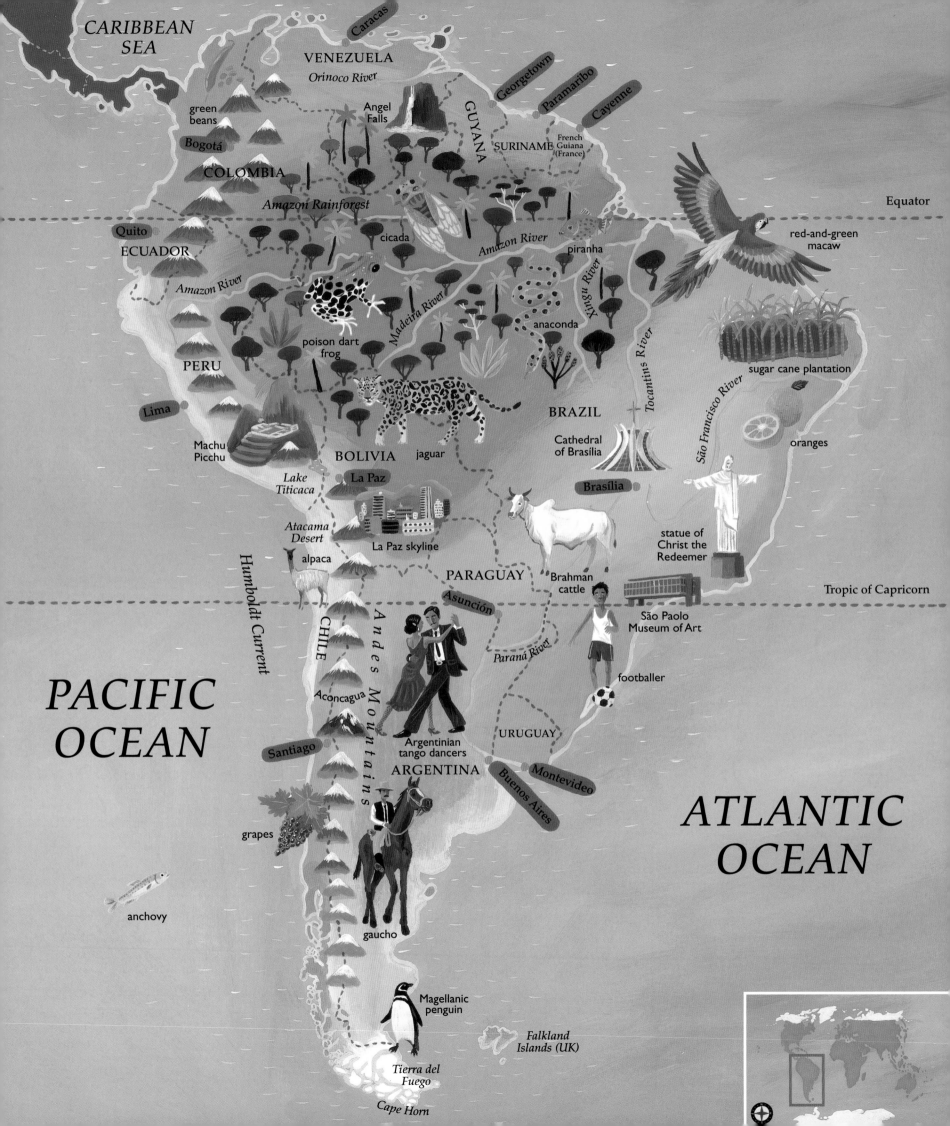

CARIBBEAN
SEA

Caracas

VENEZUELA
Orinoco River

green
beans

Angel
Falls

GUYANA

Georgetown

Paramaribo

Cayenne

Bogotá

SURINAME

French
Guiana
(France)

COLOMBIA

Amazon Rainforest

Equator

Quito

red-and-green
macaw

ECUADOR

cicada

Amazon River

piranha

Amazon River

Madeira River

Xingu River

poison dart
frog

anaconda

Tocantins River

sugar cane plantation

PERU

São Francisco River

Lima

BRAZIL

oranges

Machu
Picchu

jaguar

Cathedral
of Brasília

*Lake
Titicaca*

BOLIVIA

La Paz

Brasília

statue of
Christ the
Redeemer

*Atacama
Desert*

La Paz skyline

alpaca

PARAGUAY

Brahman
cattle

Tropic of Capricorn

São Paolo
Museum of Art

PACIFIC
OCEAN

Humboldt Current

CHILE

A n d e s   M o u n t a i n s

Asunción

Paraná River

footballer

Aconcagua

Argentinian
tango dancers

URUGUAY

ATLANTIC
OCEAN

Santiago

ARGENTINA

Montevideo

Buenos Aires

grapes

anchovy

gaucho

Magellanic
penguin

*Falkland
Islands (UK)*

*Tierra del
Fuego*

Cape Horn

Glossary

atmosphere: The mixture of gases that surround the earth.

carbon balance: The balance between the amount of carbon released into the atmosphere and the amount that is stored in the oceans, the soil and vegetation. For example, felling the trees of the rainforests creates an imbalance; planting trees helps to restore it.

carbon emissions: The release of carbon into the environment in gaseous form, in particular by heating and lighting, industrial processes, agriculture and transportation.

"clean" energy: Energy that is generated in a way that does not pollute the atmosphere.

climate: The prevailing weather conditions over a time period, including temperature, precipitation (rain, hail or snow) and wind speeds.

climate change: The change in climate over time. Climate change can be caused by natural cycles and events, and by the greenhouse gas emissions of humankind.

conservation: The management of the natural environment in such a way that wildlife and plants are protected from damage or extinction.

diverse/diversity: Made up of many different, interconnecting elements, like pieces of a puzzle. The earth is defined by its diversity because it is home to many varying forms of life, each of which depends on the others for its existence.

ecosystem: A community of interacting plants and animals, small and large, within their particular environment.

environment: The surroundings and conditions in which a person, plant or animal lives.

fossil fuel: Fuels found underground, which have been formed from the fossilization of living things like plants and animals. The main fossil fuels are petroleum, natural gas, coal and peat.

geothermal: Relating to the internal heat of the earth. In volcanic areas, it can be used as an energy source.

global warming: The increase in temperature of the earth's atmosphere.

"green": A way of describing the activities and philosophy of those concerned with protection of the environment.

greenhouse effect: The trapping of the sun's warmth in the earth's lower atmosphere. The release of carbon dioxide from burning fossil fuels into the atmosphere contributes to a "greenhouse effect," which leads to global warming.

greenhouse gas: A gas that contributes to the greenhouse effect by absorbing infrared radiation.

habitat: The place where a plant or animal lives.

hemisphere: Half of the globe.

hydropower: The generation of electricity from flowing water.

natural resource: A material or living being that occurs or exists naturally on Earth without human technology.

projection: The representation of a three-dimensional object on a flat surface. We use projections to create maps.

radiation: Energy emitted in the form of waves or particles, including the energy given off by the sun.

sustainability: The ability to use natural resources in such a way that they are not depleted.

threatened species: A species that is in danger of becoming extinct in the near future.

Sources

Clover, Charles. *The End of the Line: How Over-fishing is Changing the World and What We Eat.* London: Ebury, 2004.

Dow, Kirstin and Thomas E. Downing. *The Atlas of Climate Change: Mapping the World's Greatest Challenge.* Earthscan Atlas Series. London: Earthscan, 2011.

Encyclopedia of Animals. London: Dorling Kindersley, 2006.

Fortey, Richard. *The Earth: An Intimate History.* London: HarperCollins, 2004.

Geographica: World Atlas and Encyclopedia. Potsdam: H.F. Ullmann, 2008.

Girling, Richard. *Rubbish!: Dirt on our hands and crisis ahead.* London: Eden Project, Eden Project Books, 2005.

Hulme, Mike. *Why We Disagree About Climate Change: Understanding Controversy, Inaction and Opportunity.* Cambridge: Cambridge University Press, 2009.

Kunzig, Robert and Wallace S. Broecker. *Fixing Climate: The story of climate science – and how to stop global warming.* London: Green Profile, 2008.

Pearce, Fred. *The Last Generation: How nature will take her revenge for climate change.* London: Eden Project Books, 2006.

Pollan, Michael. *The Omnivore's Dilemma.* London: Penguin, 2006.

Rahmstorf, Stefan and Katherine Richardson. *Our Threatened Oceans.* London: Haus, 2007.

Roberts, Callum. *The Unnatural History of the Sea: The Past and Future of Humanity and Fishing.* London: Gaia Books Ltd., 2007.

The Times Comprehensive Atlas of the World. London: HarperCollins, 2005.

Walker, Gabrielle and Sir David King. *The Hot Topic: How to Tackle Global Warming and Still Keep the Lights on.* London: Bloomsbury, 2008.

Wilson, Edward O. *The Diversity of Life.* London: W. W. Norton, 1993.

Worldwatch Institute. 2009 *State of the World: Confronting Climate Change.* London: Earthscan Ltd., 2008.

Index of Countries and Capitals

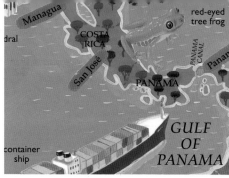

Barefoot Books
2067 Massachusetts Ave
Cambridge, MA 02140

Graphic design by Louise Millar, London
Cartography by Stephen Raw, Manchester, UK
Reproduction by B & P International, Hong Kong
Printed in Malaysia
This book was typeset in Fligerish, Minya Nouvelle, Palatino and Rockwell
The illustrations were prepared in acrylics

ISBN 978-1-84686-333-2

Library of Congress Cataloging-in-Publication Data:
is available under LCCN 2010053980

9

Editor's Note: As there are many different ways to spell and name the places of the world, for consistency we conformed to the spellings in *The Times Comprehensive Atlas of the World.*

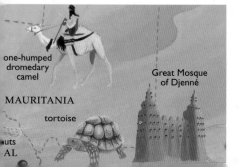